Home
Away
Elsewhere

Poems
by
Vaughan
Rapatahana

Proverse
Hong
Kong

D1715116

HOME, AWAY, ELSEWHERE is a poetry collection in three parts. *Home* is events, situations, descriptions, and attitudes about Hong Kong, which is now Vaughan's home. *Away* contains poems about events, situations, descriptions, and attitudes about Aotearoa-New Zealand, in particular from a (marginalised) Maori perspective, and also about all the other places where Vaughan has lived and visited, including: The Republic of Nauru, Brunei Darussalam, The People's Republic of China, Australia, The United Arab Emirates (UAE), The Philippines. *Elsewhere* is emotions (the entire gamut), relationships (marriages, family, friends), deaths (parents, children), reflections – some wry – and is not specifically tied to physical locations.

VAUGHAN RAPATAHANA is a New Zealander who has lived for many years in a variety of countries and now lives and works in Hong Kong. He published two collections of poetry in the 1980s: *Down among the Dead Men* and *Street Runes*. After a lapse of two decades, in 2008 Vaughan returned to poetry and has recently been published worldwide, for example, Aotearoa-New Zealand, Australia, France, Hong Kong, Malaysia, The Philippines, Thailand, the United Kingdom, and the U.S.A. In 2009 he was long-listed (a semi-finalist) for the inaugural Proverse Prize. Vaughan is Poetry Editor for MAI Review Journal, a leading online academic journal specializing in the work of indigenous writers, and he is a member of the New Zealand Poetry Society. Vaughan has a PhD in Existential Literature and Philosophy from the University of Auckland. Vaughan's heritage is Maori and he affiliates to the TeAtiawa iwi (tribe). His wife Leticia is from the Philippines and they are a multilingual household.

Proverse Prize Semi-Finalist, 2009

Home
Away
Elsewhere
Poems

*Semi-finalist,
inaugural
Proverse Prize*

Vaughan
Rapatahana

Proverse
Hong
Kong

Home, Away, Elsewhere
by Vaughan Rapatahana
2nd pbk ed. pub. in Hong Kong by Proverse Hong Kong, May 2016
Copyright © Proverse Hong Kong, May 2016.
ISBN: 978-988-8228-48-5

1st published in pbk in Hong Kong by Proverse Hong Kong,
22 November 2011.
Copyright © Proverse Hong Kong, 22 November 2011.
ISBN 978-988-19932-2-9

Enquiries: Proverse Hong Kong, P. O. Box 259, Tung Chung Post
Office, Tung Chung, Lantau, NT, Hong Kong SAR, China.
E-mail: proverse@netvigator.com
Web site: www.proversepublishing.com

The right of Vaughan Rapatahana to be identified as the author of this work has been asserted by him in accordance with the Copyright, Designs and Patents Act 1988. The right of James Norcliffe to be identified as the author of 'Preface' has been similarly asserted.

Proverse Hong Kong

British Library Cataloguing in Publication Data (1st print edition)

Rapatahana, Vaughan.
  Home, away, elsewhere.
  1. Hong Kong (China)--Poetry. 2. Rapatahana, Vaughan--
  Homes and haunts--Poetry. 3. Emotions--Poetry.
  I. Title
  821.9'2-dc22

  ISBN-13: 9789881993229

Preface

If life were to imitate art, then Vaughan Rapatahana should be a very tall, extremely skinny person, ever reaching and unsteadily lurching. Vaughan is not anything like this, of course. In person, he is all solidity, firm of voice and sure of grasp.

His poems, though, snake down the page one word or brief phrase at a time, clambering single space or double space in search of their resolution. Nor is he content to strip sentences to their single constituents but often he dismantles the words themselves, with e.e. cummings or Lewis Carroll-like abandon, stretching words, angling them, or stepping them letter by letter down the page. For the most part, conventional punctuation is eschewed. Meaning is unpacked through lineation, spacing and the device of *graphonics*. Graphonics, as the word implies, is where the shape or size of the letters in a word indicates the desired sound or meaning of the word. The device, while as old as Laurence Sterne, found its true home in comic books. Remember the lettering of the *wham, bam, zowie* sound effects in Disney and Marvel? While not going as far as Walt or Stan Lee, Vaughan employs a wide range of font sizes, letters in bold or italics, superscript, underlining and capitals to establish both his sound effects and his meaning. All this might sound a little disconcerting and it may take a moment or two to come to grips with Vaughan's singular style, a style he is steadfastly loyal to throughout *Home, Away, Elsewhere*. However, as happens with *A Clockwork Orange* or *Riddley Walker,* you quickly adapt to the tics of language and layout and the voice of the poet soon speaks to you clearly, for beneath their surface the poems are direct and accessible, paradoxically perhaps, plain-speaking and without subterfuge or pretension.

I first met Vaughan fifteen or so years ago in one of the two staff common rooms of what was then known as *Sekolah Menengah Jerudong*, later re-named *Sekolah* Menengah

Sayyidina Hussain, a secondary school some miles out of Bandar Seri Begawan in Brunei Darussalam. I had just arrived in the country after taking up a contract with the Centre for British Teachers (CfBT), a U.K. educational service company based in Reading. Vaughan, also with CfBT, had already been in Brunei for some months.

As it happened, I was allocated the work-desk next to Vaughan in the large open-plan room. Also, as it happened, we were the only two New Zealanders in the small English department, of about seven or eight teachers. As New Zealanders, we had, of course, much in common, but we had many differences as well. I was born in Greymouth on the west coast of the South Island and raised in Christchurch. Vaughan was born in Patea, Taranaki and raised in Manawatu and then Mangere, subsequently spending a lot of time in Te Araroa on the East Coast of the North Island, a region later made famous by the film *Whale Rider*. I was Pakeha; Vaughan has a Maori background and is heavily imbued with the language and culture of his people. The city I am most familiar with is Christchurch; Vaughan has spent much time in Auckland. My background was narrowly educational and literary; Vaughan had had a much more eclectic range of experiences.

What we did share, though, was a love of literature and writing. I was pleasantly surprised that my name as a writer was not unknown to Vaughan. He told me of the novel he had written and was trying to get published. We talked of New Zealand writers and literary magazines. Within a year or two, Vaughan returned briefly to Auckland University's English Department to defend his doctoral dissertation on the English writer Colin Wilson. And shortly thereafter his PhD was conferred. Colin Wilson, most famous for his book *The Outsider*, a study of such writers as Sartre, Camus, Lawrence, and others, was required reading for those of us who were educated in the 60s, one of a pantheon of counter-culture figures such as the existentialists and the angry young men. Although Wilson's star has waned in the years since, it seemed appropriate to me that he should have appealed to Vaughan, something of an outsider himself, who seemed on the surface a collection of contradictions and take-no-prisoner attitudes. There was plenty to take an attitude to, of course. Vaughan has fun with the old Noel Coward line in his *stranded in Senkurong*:

> *here*
> *it is ALWAYS*
> *hot*
>
> *too much*
> *for orang putih*
> *to stroll*
> *in the midday sun;*
> *even*
> *the*
> *maddest   one*
> *feigns*
> *sanity*

Brunei had attracted all manner of interesting outsiders.

After we left Brunei (I left first, Vaughan replacing me as Head of Department), Vaughan and I continued to correspond from time to time and we would meet on his occasional visits home. After Brunei, Vaughan spent some time first in the People's Republic of China, then in Hong Kong, before returning to New Zealand. After this, he spent almost a year in the United Arab Emirates before returning to Hong Kong, where he lives now.

Occasionally, with an e-mail note, Vaughan would attach two or three of the poems he had begun to write, asking for my opinion. I had been for many years the poetry editor for *Takahē* Magazine. As he grew more sure of his voice, Vaughan began to formally submit some of these poems and I was happy to publish a selection. Since then, his work has appeared in many literary journals in

New Zealand and beyond, including *Landfall*, New Zealand's oldest and most prestigious literary periodical. The result has been a growing body of work the best of which has been gathered together in this volume.

Vaughan has led a nomadic life now for many years, moving between Aoteoroa-New Zealand and South East Asia particularly, but further beyond from time to time. What to others might be exotic has become Vaughan's diurnal reality. Vicissitudes of place too have been accompanied by vicissitudes of circumstance. Significantly, the first section of the book largely located in Hong Kong is given the title *Home*. Not for him the postcard poems of the occasional traveller, Vaughan's observations are grounded in the deeper knowledge of those who live, eat, sleep and work in a given landscape. The poems, as a result, are more felt, more tangible. Moreover they are poems with attitude. The work is passionate, uncompromising and sardonic. In case this suggests a darkness, and there is darkness here, I should add that there is also wit in abundance and a playfulness in language and thought that is at times laugh-out-loud funny.

Vaughan's love of language is also seen in his vocabulary. He has a magpie love of the glittering word, the obscure word, and he loves to play with these treasures and to tease out their meanings and echoes, to alliterate with them, and even at times dismember them in pursuit of the most telling resonance, visual or sound effect. He mixes these with the colloquial, the telling juxtaposition, and the odd surprising image, into a language he has made his own. It is a compelling voice and Vaughan uses it skilfully to tell us his stories, make his often pungent points, and take us places few of us have seen.

Towards the end of the collection there is a poem called *mongrel poems* and in it Vaughan asks:

whatever happens
to all
those

un leashed
mongrel   poems...

Well, this is what happens to them. Here they are in all their fecund variety and it's great that Vaughan has unleashed them.

James Norcliffe
Church Bay, New Zealand

Acknowledgements

Back cover photo by Leticia Canlas.
Front cover sketches by Pauline Canlas Wu.

Author's Introduction

Writing poems for me is religion: an attempt to impose some sort of thin form onto the massive chaos that I sense lurks just beneath. I have to write to stay sane – these poems express what I am, and what I also think people are, within. They cannot be mere academic or literary exercises. They are lived experiences, I guess.

So I do not write to any set forms but do attempt to utilize type face/formats/fonts to shape what a poem looks like on a page to reflect what I attempting to say.

I would also like to think that many of these poems could and should be performed at live readings. Poetry, for Maori especially, is an oral art. To me poetry is a form of the blues and has to be presented to be best appreciated.

Vaughan Rapatahana
June 2011

Table of Contents

Home, Away, Elsewhere 13

ELSEWHERE

HOME

Mongkok lane[1]

marquee
words –

sharded
episodes

in someone   else's
life
sentence –

lie

piece meal
crumbs

as
the
footpath
beckons

further along.

a
stray
gweilo,

leper-like

tastes
the
sordid
elbows
of
the
dried

fishmongers,

themselves
dessicated,

tasteless,
foregone
conclusions,

the grime-water
sluts
itself
through
his
plaintive
shoe

and

pigeons
foul
in
token
genuflection,

seeking

some
pre-text
of
daily bread.
rancid
rain –

self-important –

a

late
apostrophe
to afternoon.

New Territory English[2]

Kwok Li
     dozzzes,

bushy head d
       r
         o
           o
            p
             e
              d,
would not matter
awake:

knows no more,
cares
even
less.

some
     other
         gweilo

always

glibs & goes,

while

Shakespeare

never

came at all.

Mr Pang –

deskbound –

dreams
      downs
             t
             a
             i
             r
             s,

new N.E.T.
        needed:

(so what)

only

his
      roses
on a windowsill

      in
Wan Chai

slip
^   his defences.

```
       r
    i   i
asp     ng
```
panel chair
can't
proply
pronounce
properly

&
Kwok Li
still
snoozes
                any   way.

no
one
uses English
                        here
no
one
ever
will.

new territory 1,
english 0

climbing out of Tuesday[3]

climbing out of Tuesday,

brains limp in a
schoolbag
I
foisted
one year,

shunted home
past
the
s p r e a d e a g l e
used condom
condominiums,

sy nc op at ing
round
those
same
 5
dogs,

canine
aliens
s p r a w l e d,

a set of satay
on an
ogre
platter,

another
few dollars
swiped,

whole
from

greedy
octopus,

while
inside
mass
breaths redolent
of
a fishwife's apron

&

the *pak paks'*
burnt
lips
from butts
gone wrong

eviscerate
my
gweilo
nostrils.

climbing out of Tuesday

the sky
a misnomer,
a blatant lie
(no one can sight it)

as the

fancy dress
party
of the
uninformed
uniformed
clatters
ever on.....

& the doors

shut
behind
like
poh pos'
mouths;

more shaky
every day.

bent man, kowloon

head
    d
       o
          w
            n

gerontion,
otiose,

hat
   less,

slices
   puddles
as
troubadour
splices
   rhyme,
               excluded/deluded,

fixates in
rumbling
ramblings

spluttered
solely to
himself,

umbrella
   less,

un accompanied,

his

strum
of
              occluded
dribblings

pool
lachrymose
in
slowmo
flux

as
caterwaul
mewls
around.

a
slim
ganglionate

yawl

slewing
      so faaaar   off-course,

      his
      sail
       a
trenchant trench coat
quacking –

as ripped
as he:

a thin scar
mildly
knouting

surfaces
of
our
sinewy
skein,
as
our $$ $$ gaze
scorches on,

tunnel
vision

                                        inviolate

in the
churlish
gale.

T.S.T.[4]

this nocturne morass
   of hawkers
       hawking

'foot massage'
    &
'copy watch'

i   n   t   e   r   p   o   l   a   t   e   s

the dusky air,
        the braggart lights

   a
poly mor phous
  massing

       s i d le s

in   some

i   n   t   e   r   m   i   n   a   b   l   e
nincompoop

eddy:
the tailor man
    needles,

the 'chicken'
    squawks,
as

commuters
sidewalk
zomboid.

a washing machine,
                    all colours mixed:

this is

Tsim Sha Tsui

on any
given night:

fairground,
          playground,
                    beggarman,
                              thief.

Home, Away, Elsewhere   31

Tin Yan blues[5]

o   u   t   h   e   r   e   in
T   I   n   Y   a   n

           floor
       21st
    the
  on
up

if blessed
you
might
    just
      spy
the
ghost
that is

Shenzhen

skulking
somewhere
o   v   e   r
t   h   e   r   e.
she douses
noodles
in Tabasco,
layering
like
a bridal cake,

spooning rice
scatters
into
bogus

bowls

in dry
doses

under dead fans,

tells me about her husband
who shrugged off
to
that same
spectral
city –

only
glimpsed
when
the sky
tilts

&

she is
not so
busy scouring
gweilo
floors
free
of spilled
soy
slurped
by
sleazebag
spouses –

'left me with the kids'

Home, Away, Elsewhere   33

'seven years ago' –

I grasp her
hybrid
calque

      above
the quiet moans
&
suppurating
        groans

from d
     o
       w
          n the *wizened*
hall;

her cached
eyes
another
social welfare
cipher,

each
second
a trove
for fatal
fall/
charcoal pall…

one more
synapse
in

the
drear

pulse
drumming

this maven
of
sorrow.

Got the Tin Yan blues, baby
got me so bad I can't call
got the Tin Yan blues, baby
miracle I stay alive at all

Tuen Mun Foreign Language[6]

a mad madrigal:

paper flowers curl in
                the vestibule,
robotic marking
clockwork drills,

the thin 'aircon'
susurrus:

staff
skinned
in opera masks;
the doomed dancers
swirl
in this
 d e m e n t e d
dervish,

        over
spilled   ^   from
another
crumbling
distant
panopticon:

Albion
oh so
                        alien

to
these   other

```
              h r
           g     i
         i         s
         h         e
```

prisons

```
         tel
cas           lated
```

around
our
pedant
cells

Hong Kong, 2010[7]

         stuck
          in
         Ho Tin,
as the smog skulks,

the perennial clitter-clatter
of the
lambent light-rail

& that stoic perambulation
of the feet feet feet

plodding ever footsore
to circadian
drudgery
in some grieving
office
tower
                                   la*mb**aste***d
              behind
              over-
    b   u   r   d   e   n   e   d
              apartments
              meltedinto
  s   w   a   GG   e   r   i   n   g
         MASS.

bereft of scope,

a tunnel-vision periphrasis:
money/money/money/money.

a sort of stringent Hell
for millions;

braaaaaaaggadocio
buried alive
in dystopian maze
& diasporic haze;

our sole epiphany –
perhaps –
a smarmy bun
on that
sole
free day
fluked
once
a
year…

just another chinese girl[8]

she
was
　　　just
a n o t h e r
chinese girl.

part of a phylum,
a phalanx,
a flock

　　hair
　　straight
in　　　　bangs,

fish-hooked
l
o
n
g
down
past
ears,

the same black
spectacles
everyone
wears,

　　　dreamt up
on a conveyor belt
　　near
　　　Shenzhen;

         stocking legs,
      a Mexican wave
    festooned
 in boots'
    mass-circuit
       tromping

uniform ubiquity

at every MTR
at every mall
in every 7/11
/this urban s p r a w l

she
was
                                    just
another
chinese girl,

desperate   to   desert

behind
        the doppelganger
        grin:

fibrillating
synapses
clenching,
jerking,

these
harlequin
troopers
clandestine,

  lurking…

Home, Away, Elsewhere   41

To Shu Li in December[9]

I'm

missing

you,
and
it's

merely

Wednesday.

outside

jing cha
sirens
justly
deride
this

selfish
sent
i
ment

&

the sky's
not
taking
sides.

discipline Li
is

SHOUTING

snidely
at some

doomed

junior
suspect

– had

no

break
fast –

mind
absent,

while
the sun
preens
itself
in
smoggy
mirrors,

and won't
make up
its
mind.

the

other

staff
room

cometscollide
in
their

own
elliptic
gambits,

brains
and
mouths
a
s
k
e
w,

&

I'm
stalled
in
a
corner

box;

the show pony,
perhaps,

as
I
yearn for
your

presence,

enough
to
fret

about

tomorrow...

Pachyderm words[10]
Oral examiners meeting, Yau Ma Tei, 2009

on stage

the bullshit
s p e w s:
an ELEPHANTINE
roar
incessant

we are all
far too old
to hear
such
clumsy
pedantry,

crouched
awkward
on silly
stools,
clumped
e   n   f   i   l   a   d   e   d
on sterile floor

kiddy talk
lambastes
our ears;
the effluence
s p i l l i n g   ever   on,
basting
us
into

torpid
sub
    mission

flick the boxes
scribe the pages
guffaw on prompt

no *mahouts* us:
mere
clumps
of dried dung
ready to

d
  r
    o
      p.

West rail distance[11]

        arm
around   you,

slunk
d
  e
   e
      p
in   sleep

      on
my   shoulder,

as West rail
stole us
home

to
tin shui wai,

l o n g from
tsim sha tsui;

a   thought
    strode
my   mind –
that
we were

there:

finally
conjoined,

en route lifelong.

Home, Away, Elsewhere   48

but,

when

I
slipped
closertokiss,

surreptitious,

your *speedy twitch*

away

merely

dovetailed our d i s t a n c e.

still

some   way   to   go,

as the train

ceased,

with
us

un coupled.

Xi'an times[12]

hellacious
black,
the colour,
of skies,

season
    indeterminate...

it might be Spring:

one would
never
know.

(they kept the weather under wraps.)

those
thin
coal-inspired
flecks,
            up
snorted   ^
frozen   nostrils,

as one
cycled
on icicled
days,

a reminder
of what might be

should
the penumbra
ever
wink
enough

to show
the scrawny butts,
shared sputum,
grafted
solid
to
snapped
pavement.

(they billed us automatic heating.)

& when
the bike
was pinched,
I stumbled
the mire,
feeling my way
myopic,

never sure
where
Xi'an
went,

where it wanted
to
go.

looking back, a kiwi[13]

this
flight
    less
bird,
nestled
    in China,
squints
Aotearoa
askance

at that
                  his *whenua*,

drip-fed
worms of
news,

m
  u
    t
      t
        e
          r
            s:
too much punching
too much piss,

pockets of savagery
in the w i d e r
overcoat,
woven
    from
too much macho muck
squirming the veins,
from

Home, Away, Elsewhere   52

            Hokianga
        to
        Hokitika/
    Haast
    and
beyond…

what
is wrong
with you
my brothers
aue taku tuakana
&
my sisters
aue taku tuahine

as you slay   *tamariki*
    murder   *manuhiri*,

as you flail and fail
yourselves;
diurnal
subornation.

ashamed,
I
sl   i   nk
naked
into by   ways,
drawing on
assumed
identity,

melding
a new fresco,
another array
of plumage.

Home, Away, Elsewhere   53

never heard of league
or weetbix–
    x
fle ^ ing
tattooed
bic eps
over   here.

while
Kai Moana
Is just
one
more
corrupt
cadre
chair
brought
to bare.

AWAY

Death in Kitakyushu, 2007[14]

He had no news;

the
slim
edifice
that
was
his
day
had
dried

up

some
time
ago

with the rest.

No news.
No food.
No money.

his neighbours
had part-time
glimpsed
his thinness,

his wider eyes
engorged
by no breakfast
no tea
no dinner,

as they

   sc   utt   led
                by

bereft

railed straight
to their
next
      station,

         no
detours.

emaciation
starves your eyes
anyway:
nothing to read,
nothing to read
with.

the FAT bastard
down at Welfare
blinked
as he dug into
another
layer of
sushi,

farted,

flicked
his manly eyes
meanly
at the pile

of papers
curling
their
denial.

He was
dying
for a rice ball.

just one.

& he did.

U.S.[15]

dishevelled,
            distraught
                        & disavowed,

a nation of
clowns

regaled

in
clumpy
harlequin

heavy
bombers
reigning

empty

nimbus
                                    over

barren

            sand,

a
side
        show

for dilettantes

a
peep
        circus

Home, Away, Elsewhere   59

of
non
    sequitur

our
Hell

our
Hades

        regnant
  yet

re
  dun
      dant/rep
   ug
nant.

pack up
shut up
give up

go home
stay home

eat your

o   b   e   s   e

burgers;

munch
your own

  shit
for a while,

entropic′
dysentery
for
a
failed

nation.

Oman sands, 2006[16]

these dromedaries

aloof,

blend
as
their desert
into
m o n o t o n o u s
dunescape,
bereft
of choice.

the   few
'trees'
poseurs
aghast
as
the straight-snake highway
quivers ever on

headless

on Oman sands
one could die for weeks

before the
              next
                        dishdashad
beards

en route
– maybe –
to Ibri
might oblige
your dusty corpse

with a sneer

Ho Chi Minh City, 2008[17]

no McDonalds here.

the

     only

Americans

I saw,

simulacrum of

Uncle HO,

palimpsest

pin –
    pricked

t h r o u g h o u t

Saigon's *scootered* sanctum:

KFC colonels.
the head, the beard,
the stare.

should have sent a regiment in the first place,

better chicken
                   than
                     dead…

Karon Beach, Phuket[18]

there's
a l w a y s
a
                  lonely
girl
s
 lu
  nk
on
some
bare-board
stoop,
 watching
gays gambol,
as
tattooed Germans
romp obese,
and
   the
tuk tuk camarilla
p r o w l;

her saturnine eyes
lacerate so brightly,
her ivory teeth,
– thus outmaneuvered –
gridlock into grin
for those
farang
who
may
pay
for any ware/anywhere {she chooses}
to
share

Home, Away, Elsewhere

Topside, Nauru[19]

like one-armed
drownings,
these
scarred
escutcheons

crash
through the quaky crust,
dusty,

in no clear
pattern

some
      stalk
             others

a   few
                    adrift,

even more

abandoned;

all   eyeless.
doomed.

there is <u>nothing</u> else here

frigate birds stay away,

even the leaves have left

      gg
just ja^^ed
monoliths:
dead men.

expedition
         over –

stone surrender
to the indefectible
sun

stranded in Sengkurong[20]

here
it is ALWAYS
hot

too much
for *orang putih*
to stroll
in the midday sun;
even
the
maddest one
feigns
sanity.

rather,
they snidely
    duck
    under
    aircon
    ducts,
the false
stream
channeled
fulsome
on sweaty
frames.

here
there
is no respite,
only
endlesssummer:
thin wafts
of evil heat
        g,
      n
   i
  s
 i
r

genies
released
from
bottles
   snuck
back
from
Limbang,

their
sole
succour.

in Sengkurong

gaudy
   snakes
      play
        in
          the
        LONG grass
as
these suckers
pray
to   another
god
for

       release

from
this
furnace,

before
      their
      final
      flips
      to
hell.

pissed in Pampanga[21]

pissed in Pampanga,
seven *San Miguels*
have comotosed me,

after Mrs Canlas'
fine satay
first flayed me indecent.

others lie sleeping,
splintered s e p a r a t e,
some sort of siesta
fugue state.

rictus sun glimpses
us,
refugees,
barricaded
from any
Disney World,

while we wink
                sideways,
as the *adobo* blinks
back slyly;
rice-festooned,

cocooned in *caldareta.*

we remain
pissed in Pampanga.

filipino fling[22]

quake

that
liquid
     flash
of
leonine
  eyes,

the
cupolaed
      dash
of
inner
  thighs –

essential
ingredients
for
a
filipino
fling.

seize
this
quick
    effervescent

   s
  a *m,*
 p
s
speeeeding
      toward
         stasis:

perhaps

a
            palladium
of
promise…

more
likely,

a mix

you'll
never

quaff…

Jerusalem diptych, 2009[23]

bereft,

resplendent

in emptiness,

the alley

crepuscular,

circumlocutory,

invaded

its own

private parts

in pained

anomie,

the

arenaceous

walls

bent

inwards

as if to say

we'll get you
soon

regardless

of

religion,

        while

     the underlying myth

that was the

capricious
path

tripped

you into

believing

you'd soon be there:

just

a couple more

stations, only another

orison.

feeding toward catacomb;

the perimeter

        Mohammad
between
        & Jesus
was

anorexic

and just as

grave.

Sonora, Mexico, June 2009[24]

'where's God?'

anguished
the
policeman,

his grief
a moist
mirror

refracted

for all
to view.

cindered arms
cradling
a
charred
waif,

comatose,

asphyxiate
a
          takeout
from
the
selfish
blaze.

some
wailed,

some

strained

to smash

Hermosillo's
murky
gates,

charonesque
carriers
of

these lifelost

(so short
on lives)

beyond

the snaky fumes,
the furnaced air,
the hellfire pall.

'where's god?'
he
squalled,
beyond
despair

no pearly
portal

here
&
st. peter's
on
e x t e n d e d   l e a v e

where's god

indeed?

Tutuua *Urupa*, 2007[25]

mud tracks
truck
through this

long
over
grown

ragwort
            outside

the spindly
fence

we once painted

you lie
(inside)

quite deep down
                now

cement-wrapped,

no way out,

hemo ki tenei ao:

but then,

you'd already
long gone,

eh e hoa

Lost New Zealand Boy[26]

L
  O
    S
      T

new zealand boy:
he taitama ngaro

tries to find quota for
    back
biting
quandaries
of his own making;

        reared
in this skinny country,
snared
by its iniquities,

with its
bloody
        stupid
                name

some long-dead Dutchman who didn't breach
                                the beach;

he would find more sense
if we   shared

Aotearoa

Te Araroa Winter, 2008[27]

fluke
sun
today,

flat sea,

dead breeze.

a few silent
sparrows
f l e c k
the
pohutukawa;

only

sound

the waves

d
  o
   w
    n
there:

their

steady
cadence

ready
to snap
    this   still,

when
brothers
rain & wind
trundle home,

sodden,

tonight.

Matakaoa RSA[28]

age shall not weary them,

but
maybe

those
battalions
of beers
will.

Corporal Gilly
causes
   pauses

for *hazy*
reflection
on
photo-
faded
heroes,

while
the steady pall
of
roll-your-owns

shimmies

any
clearcut
sighting
of the
other side,

of the
drawn   -   out
table,
where
cuzzies
often
nuzzle.

small talk
is   l o n g-w i n d e d,

the same
saga
every Friday:

who is
here,
& who is
there,

while
someone
always
scolds
the
jukebox
into playing

another
spectral
sixties
voice.

yet

we will remember
them.

Home, Away, Elsewhere   85

blood
curls
DEEP
through
whanau,

regardless
of

demise.

last time[29]

last time
together,
we
seldom spoke,

until
i
bought
us
    pies
in
    Tolaga.

you
said
'thanks',

munching –
hungry,
i
guess –

        after all
your
mahi
in
our
kitchen,

back home
up
   the
     Coast.

we
hit the airport,
i
asked
you
to signal,
a.o.k.

last time
i
saw
you
alive, son.

a half-smile,
thumbs up,
through
sliding doors,
bereft
of cleaning.

next
we
met,
you
were
dead,

stiff

    in
a pinebox.

still saying nothing.

we
should have
said more
on
that
trip.
together.

between bards[30]

pre-dawn,

I departed Jim's
Otautahi
abode,

an   isolate
trinket on a
bicuspid coast,

and
graunched back
into
southern
e   s   c   a   p   a   d   e:

the snowflooded hills
a sulky doppelganger
of my
own inner
              nts
          ie
      ad
gr
the road rode on,
shamelessly
simulating
direction

as   the

few

others who
could be bothered

Home, Away, Elsewhere   90

to be alive that day
fluctuated past me,
fibrillating
spasms
from dead
erections.

hours passed = madmen
released sane =
there was no crux to them –

and in this cloven crease
of time,
I was silent.

Timaru arrived,
dishevelled
and left again
no worse for wear,
while
her autumn leaves
golliwogged in
dying drains.

it was as **night**
killed again,
I sniffed
Dunedin

&
finally,

somehow

a thin shard of sense
struck back –
a spindly blade

in my
stringy ribs –
to tell me
where I was,
no longer
stabbing
why.

at David's home
a gulp of wine,
a chortle
of *kai*

some rumpled sleep
before
the
next inebriate
glissade,

the scurrilous whip
of the nascent chill
speaking an eager
winter
the further
south
I spilled,

poleward,

between bards
and
b e y o n d
any

waft

of return.

Home, Away, Elsewhere   92

Opotiki schoolmate, 40 years on[31]

he seemed happy enough
locked
in
his own
crowded
sanctum,

peeled grape eyes,
somewhat   askew

the hair now frostbitten,
and a paunch
to die for

form four
tattooed
fingers
splayed
in roll-your-own
spasms

&

a
permanently silly grin
spread like
runny butter
across
his stubbled
chin

if I didn't know him better
I'd swear
his rheumy
greeting curse

Home, Away, Elsewhere   93

was
heartfelt

and not

the lexicon
of a lost soul
downgrading,

years adrift,
tokeing
too many
flaccid doobies
and
cheap cardboard
vino
spilled
from
the corner store.

where we used to meet up

Hori, me,

and Macca,

the brown boys
drowning in
a
sea
of white.

Pakaraka, '81[32]

up   Smiths   Road,
once
the
dust
had
                                died,

you might
have
seen
the
rumpled roof
corrugations,
slou
        ch
                ing
as
the
                foun
        der
ing
piles
carped
ceaselessly
uNdernEaTh,

bus ted
weatherboard
here   &   there,
we soon
revamped.

Hone's
splurging
paintbrush

Home, Away, Elsewhere   95

a
stalwart
apostate:

made a home
listening to Jimmi,
warm by
the crumpled
grate,
cooking
hoary logs
fetched
from that
fetid
swamp,
ashes
splayed
in homage
to the
meniscus
moon.

&

when
we shot
that neurotic
cur

– a stray
you salvaged –

for
worrying
Jim O's
stock,

there
was
always
another
patch-
    up
job
on
the
list

limp
    ing from
        the
           oily wall.

up   Smiths   Road,

me some
longhair
tranche
from
a
mislaid
file,
you

Wahine Kino
burnt
us
        out,
frying chips
on
the drowsy
stovetop,

the febrile

walls
laughing
in their
quick
collapse,
the flames
that ravenous
dog
melting
all
with
its
scabrous tongues.

so
was time to move   on.

only
these
wrinkled
words,
scurrying   like   the   washhouse
rats   across   a

                                        littered   page,
some faint recall
of
Pakaraka,
'81,

when Sir James
blessed
us
all
with *whaikorero*
that
stand

Home, Away, Elsewhere   98

faaaaaaaaaaaaaaar
longer;

kei whea te komako e ko?

indeed.

Papatoetoe summer grass[33]

1.

as the lawn m o w e r
pu r r r ed,
                    scything
centrifugal
in

fake
     abandon,

he hitched

                    his wrap-around
                    walk shorts,

a Farmer's sale tartan
of rapid blue blushes,

further to his fetid groin,
and stepped ferocious,

plastic sandals
his Mother bought in 1966
from a long-dead store

in Ponsonby;

Masport scimitars
torturing

the lank brown blades

into skanky rows,

as if
they cared anyway.

2.

next door Mr Pou

glimpsed over
the unsteady wall.

Lion Red
in his sweaty maw,
a faint grimace
     under
     s l u g
    plastic fan,

thinking
'screw that, man' –

scratched his balls
through
broken
underpants –

the motley weeds   on this
side
'look better anyway':

  closersomehow

to
his   pock mark ed
       turf.

wharenui[34]

o u t   b   a   c   k

lion **red**

or some palsied surrogates

stood firm

in the arms akimbo

tribe,

circling
       the
           perimeter,

regaled

in faded-black
singlets/conjugating/
with refugee
         abattoir
       boots

       never
     returned
   14 years
before.

no more spuds
to peel

hangi ready
a while back,

dishes can
wait 'til
after

whaikorero
have stripped
senseless
those
captured
inside
the stockade;

stymied by
protocol

& age

& duty…

& hunger.

AAAaaeeeeeAA

light up
another
kai paipa

some
fellas'd
do
anything
for a feed

eh.

Aotearoa blues, baby[35]

'typical bloody Maori'

she snitched,

assuming
me
one
of her kind;

'you don't look like a Maori'

her brazen
shibboleth,
when
I protest...

[smug
  &
spiteful,
       bourgeois
        &
       blinkered.]

another
    of
      the
       ilk

= my own cousin, on the *pakeha* side =

pukes
     out

the familiar
dead

homily:

'Maori are lazy, they don't want to work'

(where?*)*

'and end up in jail anyway'

(you wonder

why? *e mohio ana ahau!*)

she
should have
known
better,

her
nasty
sneeeeeers

fulcrum
of
some
OTHER
caustic
core rage.

she
didn't intuit
my
own
inner
tube,

swell
fulminating,

just
about

ready to rupture,

r e a c h   o u t

& strangle her
in irredentist fury…

but then

'that brown one'
                    (*taku hoa wahine*)
would have been

tino
mokemoke –
                    (maybe)

– with me
            just
scratching
tats

            up
in   ^
Pare

  – where
I'm
supposed
to be.

got those damned Aotearoa blues, baby
slicing through my soul
keep a man way down under, baby
never can be whole

postcolonial boy[36]

could never
work out
what god
& the queen
had to do
with
us

mooching
through
that
bloody empiric dirge

every

morning
in school.

neither came near
us
&
our
second-hand-me-downs,
in
Mangere,

as far as
I recall.

could never
comprehend
why
CompulsoryMilitaryTraining

some crazy jingoistic suck-up –

Home, Away, Elsewhere   107

dragooned us,

                    a   d   r   i   f   t
in Waiouru,

bleary-eyed,
in
jumbo
overcoats,

gearing to
fight
viet cong

who didn't
glean where
we came from,

        only

that we
were too
damned fat
for their
cunning
tunnels.

just wanted to be
a
wild
postcolonial
                boy
    up
back
of

Whetumatarau,

eating
the blue sky
for breakfast
every
day,

unfurling
tino rangatiratanga
from that
spare-room drawer

&

floating
it
on the
hang
    mouth
c   l   o   t   h   e   s   l   i   n   e

for all
the world
to be.

Rata villa, Ngawhatu[37]

one was doing

     whe
cart   ^   els

a   c   r   o   s   s
the sunlit
compound
c   a   r   p   e   t,

infecund smile
s t r e t c h m a r k e d
as   w   i   d   e:

others
squat
forlorn
statues

  in
shaded
crannies,

their
e y e s
wine   gums
far   b e y o n d
expiry date.

If I ate
    there
I cannot recall
more
than
a TRUCKLOAD

of *ativan*
arriving
weekly,

while
my
sp lint er e   d
brain
    roiled

    k
brea in g,

b o
  r k e
        n,

abnegating x
        x
          x
            x
              x
                x
sleep.

                    after
Ngawhatu
the jigsaw
      jags

      never
quite

         gelled

again

East Coast morning[38]

sundered,

the rocks
sense
betrayal,

the
aloof
gulls

         t
       f
     o
  l
   a

wheedling,
             gyrating,
s
  w
   o
    o
     ping

    on
l i n g e r i n g
  scrap

token d r i f t w o o d
           under

as
the
scrawny
wavelets

taunt
the shore.

          up

there,

          askew
the fledgling sun,

a figure
dawdles

redolent
in
the
pohutukawa,

its
cherub
blossoms
an open
echo   echo   echo
of
his
winey
daze,

while

the *frisky*
gusts

invade,

deflowering
the

dawn.

Waima epiphany[39]

was waaay back of Kaikohe
                near
                       30 years ago,

the clapped-out
Mark IV
rumbling
like a
bruised jeremiah
on the shingle
tarmac,

forsaking
benediction

as

the gnarled 'Nam vet
we'd rescued from
the spattered tavern
hoiked acrid phlegm
from
the depths
of the back-seat dungeon
on
    to
the gorse sprayed
      clay,

while

I
pissed
fulsome
into the

greedy ditch
like
a corybantic dog

&

you
threw off
the spigots
of your entire life
until then
in eerie tears.

the stygian air
reeked
the arrogant
macoracapa
sentineled
by some fussy Anglo farmer

                                    an age before,

to neuter
us
                    seeding
our own *whenua.*

I swear
I saw
a jovian moon,
licentious in its waxing smile,
d
   i
      p
profound
just above us,

a tessellated avatar,

Home, Away, Elsewhere   117

&

its complicit star cousins
coruscated beyond
effervescent
in full five minute
spasm,

an epiphany
@ c 3.33 a.m
        on a
            glacial
                Ngapuhi
                    dawn,:

an occult glyph
unveiled.

nestles with me still
when I hear
sad cattle
bellow
as
a chill night zephyr
shakes through me
darkly;

like
battery acid
on my aging
skin.

no holy grail[40]

so
he
challenged
the cup,

trounced
the
confident
glass

tino rangatiratanga

dented
a
clov   en
nat   ion's

       ss
mi   ^   hapen

pride,

the inane
badinage
'we are all one',
pummeled
fiftyfold
by
frantic
pein;

a
side/swipe
to
    'equality',

the pasty
smirk
pulverised,

if only for a spell.

here's to
Benjamin Peri
Nathan.

america's chalice
was
never
worth $$$$$$$$$$$$$$$$$$$$$$$$$$$$$$
jousting for,

the   brew

        inside
    bitter-sweet

        &

    poison
    well-before

            his
                            lone
crusade,

                &
the *iwi*

crewed
their
craft
     oceans

ahead
     of
     this
     tramontane
         episteme.

pestilence[41]

1.

the rats
s c a r p e r e d

when james cook
endeavoured
tuuranga-a-nui,

back in
1769

[nyet nakysniki][a]

d
  o
    w
      n
  the
hawsers
scuttling,
  scum

s   i m   i n
  w m   g

          to the shore,

reaching
     reaching
         reaching
            the beach;

---

[a] *nyet nakysniki* (Russian] no rat prevention devices on ships' anchor ropes

shame
these
brig
   pariah

didn't drown
then　&　there.

  2.

they've <u>never</u> left;

a perdurable
pale
plague
meddling

clergy　clerisy　*contador*　　*conquistador*
             intra-island
       c o n t e r m i n o u s:

their canard
of
diarchic　　　　　　　　　　'sharing'

STILL

lying
l　i　n　g　e　r　i　n　g
[they try to ratiocinate their ratshit.]

  3.

There's **not** some ludic
frolic
here,

Home, Away, Elsewhere　　　　　123

there's **not** some edenic
picnic
here:

wrong
rubric

                It's not Godzone
                   Here
[more like endzone.]

    4.

hindi natutulog ang Diyos   ['the Lord never sleeps']

my Pampanga wife
soothes from afar

[rodents hoard visas they never had themselves]

et mon Dieu
I hope she's right.

These vermin nearly
                scuppered us,

lucky

nga kiore waka
breed
necrophanic

like

Home, Away, Elsewhere   124

rats
   rats   rats   rats
rats   rats   rats   rats
     rats   rats   rats   rats
     rats   rats   rats

Toa[42]

these tattooed words

    h   i   r
w   l

                forth,

curlicues
a   s   t   r   i   d   e
my hulking
chest

itself

habitat
of skin-seared
pitau

these joint
manaia,

the presumptuous
jaw,

the cowled
brow,

scorch

my
mighty
mana.
firm me to the
      soil

anchor
me

here

a
v a s t
dark
bulk

preparing
to

pounce.

james k.[43]

i selected him

       -   through the gauzy pell-mell

                   of pall mall & grey's

     10's –

in the kiwi;

           that occluded haunt,

           slatternly carpet
           thr ead ba re
           beneath
           underage feet.

magpie eyes,

his nose
      a beak,

whisker wisps
     stealing
  d   p
    e e
    into
lip   crevasse,

tussling there,

spoiling
for
a
sonnet.
faint froth
      residue, rescued
          from the frightened glass,

his
                    - dare i say it –
anorexic claws
clutched
like an all-day roost,

arm
     p   r   o   t   r   u   d   i   n   g
     from
   the dead
salvation army
   plumage
                    – suited him well, i have to say –
6 sizes
too BIG

for any lesser man.

ELSEWHERE

hey Leticia[44]
(pretty woman)

a
few
syll   a   bles

just

for
you.

hey Leticia

words churn
mud
when
I strive
to find
any

(encapsulating you.)

they *scurry* away,
stu
    mb
        ling

don't care to
know;

the little bastards
are
mortificd,

Home, Away, Elsewhere   131

fretting
they'll

never catch
you
never match
you,

they'll
mire into
pabulum

& no dictionary
will want them.
hey

Leticia

that sound

alone

is all
there
needs
to
be.

you killed me[45]

was that
smile
that
ate
me.

lips
curled
in such
a
clever
way,
my soul
swallowed
    whole

  &&
when your
slim
    fingers
lightly
snuck
my
blind
hand,

comeback
was
impossible.

siren
eyes
conveying
the
final
flaying
of my
heart.

ahhhh

you should
be
banned.

your body
is
the
death

of

mine.

thoughts of you[46]
Ki a Ereti

thoughts of you
                    keep me warm;

there is

no

snow
                    here,

yet chill

                                        drifts
                    e
              s
            i
        r

sufficient

that brisk
dank
damp,
inchoate
within,

a
smirk–
        smothering
demon,

&

as
those
wicked
sleet sheets
                    disagree
outside,

thoughts of you
sustain
          me

I love you more[47]

I love
you
more
than
all
those
other contenders,
flashing
their sprightly teeth over
lightly-licked lips,
tongues
swishing through
in sexual
derisions.

I love
you
more than
all
those
other wanna-bes,
sluicing
their rampant manes in
faint expectation
I will leap over
and finger comb those tresses;
sultry
eyes
lusting
for
promise.

I love you more
than any man
can,
more than
temptation
mounts
to
incarcerate
me
in its
widescreen
bosom,
swaying
its wanton
hips,
figuring
my demise
into
sheets
of solid satin.

I love you more
than this.

Li Shu Kai, September 2007[48]

You were taller than the others,

a head above,
yet somehow
no downward
                    glances
tarnished
your aloofness.

a sad femininity,
stranded somewhere
between
girl
& woman,
eyes scan instead
for a father
perhaps,

or at least
a loving touch
that might linger.

craving
more than
fleeting passion,
that flying night synapse,

another
rough-sawn
let-down.

You were
taller
than the rest
anyway.

an inner height,
regardless,
lifted you apart.

You will always
stand out,
sitting
gentle

in that corner.

not really missing you[49]
Kii a Ereti

not really
       missing
you,

the incessant
smoky
homage

&

checks
on dad.

Yet,
you
are here
far
more
now
you have
       gone.

wardrobe
s   p   a   c   e
&
empty
bed-side

frequent
signposts
to
your

presence,

while
the
unused
towels
clamour
far
more

for
my attention
than
they
ever did
before.

taku papa[50]

nothing much
   grew
   in
my father's
garden,
as he
drank
d
  o
    w
      n
to demise;

except

the
naughty
weeds,
the
d e a t h l e s s
rhubarb
&
flagrant
ragwort
some times always;

the compost bin
never-ending,

its
pipi shells
catseyes
    stalking,

spurned
our slim
advances.

& at the enD
even
the languid top
        soil
had given up
& s
  u
  n
  k
beneath the
old
vauxhall
he'd
circum   sized
up portage road
one   sullen   night,
          after
16 beers
too many.

no surface[51]

cannot
rake

sunny comatose verse
in carefully tilled rows,
dapper, well-watered
pansies & violets,
anemones trimmed succinct,
all laced in rhyming bows
of cleverly shoveled metaphor
and words far too big
for their gumboots
astride the polite verbal hose.

this rainbow garden
was never
gifted
me

as
I

p
  l
    u
      n
     g
the   e   topsoil

extirpating
petals,
the brightened blues
&
lavish reds,

down
to
the
gnarly
roots

d
   e
      e
        p
          e
            r

into
that
dark
barren
penumbra
of
the
savage black:

Mother's bruises
even
duskier
than
her
cheap/woolworths
sun/shades
camouflaging
the callous
hacking
of
her
husband's
sotted
fist.

god is a weasel[52]

god is a weasel,
a possum,
maybe
    a stoat.

    lying
in these autumn
shells:
leaves
dressed to kill,

god
could be
any of these.

locked in
some
undetectable
system.

so
faaar
from
our own.

bathos[53]

awash in
       bathos

we

await –

cerulean
current

a   d   r   i   f   t –

fearing

for

more.

there is no more.

tide[54]

the sea
turned
  itself
   in,

no l o n g e r
innocent
of crimes
against/humanity,

its
swashed

flume
gave   away
its tacky true
purpose

before
 baked
  armada
   of
     nubile
       babes;
languid,

their
own flotilla
of
fake
beaux,

biceps
desperate
to pose,
dry,

drowning
spurious
in   coming
swathe,

as,

conceding
all-too-late,

the
wavelets
rescinded
their
motion.

old shoes[55]

we fittogether
like
two old shoes

unrepaired
and
s p l i t a p a r t
at the soles.

well-worn and unbecoming,
slipshod and tarnished,

battered and bruised,
used and abused.

blistered & gnarled
  & tacky & raw,
splintered & punished
  & grimy and poor.

down at the heels,
scuffed at the seams,
lost in our own
meandering dreams.
we fittogether
like
two old shoes,

lying heapedtogether
in the

bottom

of someone's
cosmic
wardrobe.

too complicated[56]

too complicated,
you said

and you
were
right.

too much
en
        cumb
                rance
   thwarting
any

nascent
        bonds;

no authentic
aspect
to
our
torpid
roles

here

in this
nutty
prance

where we
stroll
like
skinny
zombies

who don't know
of death

too complicated
you said.

and

you
were
right.

encounter[57]

a
counterscrew
        turns

obliquely,

        despite.

you

reverse
all
                revolutions

with
pressure
from
those
who
would be
your
courtesans,

        in spite of.

screwing
firmly
forever

any
rampant
possibility

into

early
       demise,

aeons ahead
of any

bedding,

         without respite.

faded love[58]

faded love:

   an

    turn
  p   e
u   d

milkshake.

last

vestige

ice
   mush,

faint froth
         flecks,

your
lipmark
trace

on
   the
        edge

of my

mind.

corrupted[59]

I could have loved you
elsewise
but
the finger pointers
rally,
black tongues
lollygagged
in plagued oath,
gesticulating
wizened ganglions
like
diseased doves
in their final
death s
      w
         o
           o
              p.

I could have loved you MORE
than
any man
can,

but

for this
Boschean
frame
around us.

surrounds us
drowns us,

and I cannot plunge deep

enough
to salvage
any
of your
sharp glances
in my vague direction.

I Should Have Done More

For Blake Robertson, 23/01/76–13/10/05

I should have done more,

when you were

still

alive,

son.

I should have done
MORE.

I should have been
more
implicated –

somehow.

told you I loved you:

all that stuff
fathers tend not to do,
but always
aspire.

it is all
too late
now.

You took that
irrevocable.

P
  L
    U
      N
        G
          E.

the endgame dive
into Death

up the bastard
                b
           a
           c
         k
of cannons bloody creek.

so   v   a   s   t   l   y

alone.

shit of a way to

leave
us,
son

to blank out
life's
dis   ill   usions –
                         for you,

&
maybe

your own to it.

Here – words

dis
    i
        n
te
             gra
   t
                 e

into filler, lift dirge, pap.

my miasmatic
mantra.

I should have done more.
I should have done more.

should
have
done
so
MUCH

more.

from father through son to son[60]

from father through son to son
a cleft line
s
   c
      y
        t
           h
             e
               s

deft.

two masts
down,

I founder   adrift

through
this hellish eddy

the
                  centre
flagstaff
rotting,
ri*pp*ed
limp
mizzen

dragging
d
e
e
p
e
r
 d
   o
    w
      n

to your
accursed
silty
     lockers.

from father through   son   to   son

gone @   49
& @ 29

you never really met,

no on-board
brigandry;

rapscallion
on different
watches

yet
déjà-vu
debauchery:
conjoined your
genes,
the same
scars,
riven.

the matching
pirate
*mAdNesS#

one,
just one,

sea-scans

                    still

a   lone
lookout,

beleaguered
by
our
bandit blood

sulking
in
this
skulking
crows
nest

Where is the treasure?

There is no treasure.

There never was.

no booty
no body
but

me.

unknown poet[61]

eye sockets,

mere
figures of speech,

stare
metaphorically
at the lyric
bed;

these words
crawl,

scarab
beetles,

from
the

open

fissure
that was
mouth,
flocking
manic

through
tissued
tongue,

while
skeletal
fingers

rhyme
e r r a t i c a l l y
with

    those
fleshless
    toes

s p l a y e d

d
  e
    e
      p

beneath
dried
corpus:

the
ragged
body
of
his
work.

mongrel poems[62]

whatever happens
to all
those

un   leashed
mongrel   poems,

                              s t r a y

dog-eared
pages

   *crou*ched
bleak
sub
      mission
in some
dank
      cur sive
                  kennel

their spindle ribs
showing
through
mangy
corpus

eyes
pleading
acceptance
like
crippled
similes

comma
tails between legs,

rawboned,

forgotten
misbegotten
doggerel:

no

Such
Poetry
Contribution
Accepted.

toreador lexis[63]

these bully
     words

     m
lacerate
    e
I
parry,

without panache

pointed
thrusts,

as
they
lunge

huge
heads
   d
     o
      w
       n;
my
side   step
   inept

my
words   cape
one
glissade
tardy.

              – these snotty
              noun bastards
just
lust to kill me –

barbs
too sharp,
charged jibes
more to*read*or
than
me,

gored,
     u
   t   g,
s   mb
       l n
       i

a
bloodpool
quashed
           raging verbosity.
        beneath

mad cousin in Winter[64]

you wood-chopped

ecc en tr i c   al   ly:

windmill arms

&

s p l i n t e r   spasms

abrogating
the air

in

flail
    ^ ing

menace.

logs left

deranged

it was
then,
                only
then

the
corrugated
prisms
in my own
mental
puzzle

jackpotted

&

I

trainspotted

your

inner
dervish,

cartwheeling
backwards
over
sanity.

old Tom[65]

old Tom
sat back,

swishing his
thin lips

– the gravy-dimmed
tongue
a
frog
flicker

soon
he'd be
off
rocket launch
to lounge

c o m m a n d e e r
the controls

and
skulk

– his diminishing body

losing itself
inside the
c o u c h –

to scan
some
dopey
soap

before uncle sleep
stole in
and swept him
                                    away,

leaving

        only

                that snore
behind.

old Tom
came
around today.
he _always_ does

his
arcane
hat
clutched
the
  hall
    table
like
a small
child
a lollipop.

there is
NO
change:

dinner will be served.

A Note on Place Names

Mongkok, Kowloon, Tsim Sha Tsui, Tuen Mun, Ho Tin, Yau Ma Tei, Tin Shui Wai, Tin Yan – all Hong Kong place-names; whilst Shenzhen and Xi'an are cities in the People's Republic of China; Kitakyushu a city in Japan; Ho Chi Minh/Saigon a city in Viet Nam; Ibri a large town in Oman; Karon Beach, Phuket a tourist resort in Thailand; The Republic of Nauru is in the Central Pacific; Sengkurong a district in Brunei Darussalam; Limbang a large town in Malaysia; Pampanga a district of Luzon, Philippines; Hermosillo is in Sonora, Mexico; Jerusalam in Israel; Tutuua is the name of an *urupa* (burial ground) in New Zealand; Hokianga d, Hokitika, Haast, Te Araroa, Matakaoa d, Tolaga (Bay), Otautahi or Christchurch, Timaru, Dunedin, Opotiki, Pakaraka d, Ponsonby, Papatoetoe, Mangere, Waiouru, Whetumatarau – mountain, Ngawhatu, Waima, Kaikohe, Tuuranga-a-nui/Gisborne, Cannon's Creek – all places in New Zealand.

KEY: d = district; the rest are towns or cities.

A Note on Proper Names

Lion Red – a famous New Zealand beer.
San Miguel – a famous Philippine beer, popular in Hong Kong.

Early Responses to *Home, Away, Elsewhere*

"Vaughan Rapatahana's poems are the testament of a post-colonial wanderer. An exploration of identity politics, they move between the bicultural and bilingual context of Aotearoa New Zealand and the extraterritorial context of globalisation. They criss-cross intersections of commerce, history and culture, ranging from the United Arab Emirates to Jerusalem to Hong Kong.

Experimenting with various verse forms, his artfully woven episodes of autobiography are witty, poignant and tragic by turns, glittering with sharp insights and wry reflections as they trace narrative arcs that run between the years of adolescent idealism and post-Sixties rites of passage to more recent memories and evocations of family, friends and fellow-travellers.

These are poems freighted with combustible emotions, mingling angst and comedy and scepticism in at times fiery and haunting combinations. Sometimes dreamlike or riddling, sometimes elegiac, sometimes deliberately linguistically unstable, Vaughan Rapataha's poems make significant patterns out of the randomness of life's events and give succinct and effective voice to the peculiarly modern condition of the global nomad at once home everywhere and home nowhere."
– David Eggleton, Editor of *Landfall*, Aotearoa-New Zealand.

"...poems with attitude. ... passionate, uncompromising and sardonic. ...there is darkness here ... also wit in abundance and a playfulness in language and thought ... at times laugh-out-loud funny.... a compelling voice and Vaughan uses it skilfully to tell us his stories, make his often pungent points, and take us places few of us have seen."
– James Norcliffe, Robert Burns Fellow (2000), Aotearoa-New Zealand.

"In 'Home, Away, Elsewhere' Vaughan Rapatahana promises the deep irony/ absurdity/ reality of the new century, where home is really elsewhere and elsewhere is indeed a sort of home. Presented in relentless barrages of images, they splatter us with situations laced with a moving poetic insight — always short, sharp and revebrating with nuances and references.

These poems are pieces of an intricately interlinked multi-cultural and multi-lingual world, in which the poet must learn to live. In fact the poet relishes this confusing richness. His verses celebrate the graphic possibility of words, their visual appearance and sounds. So one must come to them with big eyes, big ears and a limitless imagination."
– Muhammad Haji Salleh, National Laureate, Malaysia.

Notes

[1] First published in *Bravado* # 16, 2009.
Gweilo – originally white devil, now a sometimes less than nice way of designating a foreigner/stranger [Cantonese]
[2] First published in *AsianCha*, August 2009.
[3] First published in *Malaysian Poetry Chronicles*, September, 2010. *Poh po* – old woman; *pak pak* – old man; *gweilo*. [Cantonese]
Octopus – fee-paying card used in Hong Kong.
[4] First published in *emanilapoetry*, September 2010.
[5] *Gweilo* [Cantonese] – see above.
[6] To be published in *English Language as Hydra* (United Kingdom, Multilingual Matters.)
[7] First published in *Malaysian Poetry Chronicles*, September 2010.
[8] First published in *The Journal*, # 33, 2011.
[9] First published in *Blackmail Press* # 22, 2008.
Jing cha – policeman [Putonghua]
[10] First published in *Malaysian Poetry Chronicles*, November 2009.
Mahout – elephant handler [Hindi]
[11] First published in *AsiaWrites*, June 2010.
[12] First published in *AsianCha*, August 2009.
[13] First published in MAI Review, September 2010.
Whenua – land; *aue taku tuakana* – oh my brothers; *aue taku tuahine* – oh my sisters; *tamariki* – children; *manuhiri* – guests; *kai moana* – seafood [Maori]
[14] First published in *Takahe* # 63, 2008.
[15] First published in STARCH # 1, 2011.
[16] First published in *Poetry New Zealand* # 39, 2009.
[17] First published in *Deep South*, November 2008.
[18] First published in *Pattaya Poetry Review*, December 2009.
Tuk tuk – small three-wheel taxi; *farang* – foreigners [Thai]
[19] To be published in *English Language as Hydra* (United Kingdom, Multilingual Matters.)
[20] First published in *The Philippine Graphic*, September 2009.
Orang putih – white man (Bahasa Melayu)
[21] First published in *emanilapoetry*, November 2009.
Adobo and *caldareta* – Filipino foods [Tagalaog]. San Miguel – famous Philippines beer.
[22] First published in *emanilapoetry*, November 2009/ *Malaysia Poetry Chronicles*, November 2009.
[23] First published in *Enamel*, June 2010.
[24] First published in *Valley Micropress*, June/July, 2009.
[25] First published in *Deep South*, November 2008.
Hemo ki tenei ao – dead in this world; *e hoa* - friend [Maori]
[26] First published in *Takahe* # 68, 2009.
He taitama ngaro – a lost boy [Maori]
[27] Vaughan Rapatahana was a featured poet in *Valley Micropress*, March 2010. This poem was first published as part of that feature.
Pohutukawa – NZ native tree [Maori]

[28] First published in *Valley Micropress*, October 2009.
Whanau – family [Maori]
[29] *Mahi* - work [Maori]
[30] First published in *The Typewriter* # 3, 2010.
Kai – food [Maori]
[31] First published in *Blackmail Press* # 27, 2010.
[32] First published in *Valley Micropress*, June 2010.
Wahine kino – literally "bad woman" – here used as a woman's name as in Maori tradition; *whaikorero* – speech; *kai whea te komako e ko?* – where then is the bellbird? (from the first line of a famous Maori saying or *whakatauki* [Maori]).
[33] First published in *Enamel*, June 2010.
[34] First published in *brief* # 39, March 2010.
Wharenui – large room for communal gatherings on Maori *marae* or communal centres; *hangi* – food traditionally cooked under the earth; *Whaikorero; kai paipa* – (smoking) cigarettes [Maori]
[35] First published in *brief* # 39, March 2010.
A report on the welfare of children in OECD member countries has found New Zealand to have the highest youth suicide rate in the developed world. The suicide death rate for Māori youth (aged 15-24 years old) in 2006 was 31.8 per 100,000, compared with the non-Māori rate of 16.8 per 100,000.
Aotearoa is Maori for New Zealand, literally land of the long white cloud; *pakeha* – white man; *e mohio ana ahau* – I know; *taku hoa wahine* – my woman friend qua wife; *tino mokemoke* – very lonely [Maori]
[36] First published in *a fine line*, July 2010.
Tino rangatiratanga – total self- determination/independence [Maori]
[37] First published in *brief* # 39, March 2010.
Pohutukawa Ativan is a medical drug for anxiety & depression
[38] First published in *Blackmail Press* # 26, 2009/*Valley Micropress*, October 2009.
[39] As note 27 above.
Whenua – land; *Ngapuhi* – Maori tribe or *iwi*
[40] *Tino rangatiratanga* – see note 36 above; *iwi* [Maori]; *episteme* – totally divergent cultural mindset and the concomitant enforcement of this [French]
[41] First published in *brief*, #41, 2010.
Contado – accountant ; *conquistador* – conqueror [Spanish]; *hindi natatalog ang Diyos* – God doesn't/never sleep(s) [Tagalaog]; *et mon Dieu* – and my God [French]; *nga kiore waka* – canoe rats [Maori]
[42] *Valley Micropress*, December 2009.
Toa – warrior; *pitau* – spiraling plant and tattoo or decorative pattern; *manaia* – spiritual guardian as traditional pattern in carving/tattoo; *mana* – prestige/presence [Maori]
[43] First published in *Blackmail Press* # 26, 2009.
[44] As note 27 above.
[45] First published in *emanila poetry*, November 2009.
[46] First published in *Blackmail Press* # 22, 2008.
Ki a – dear [Maori]
[47] First published, *Malaysian Poetry Chronicles*, September 2010.

Home, Away, Elsewhere   181

[48] First published in *Takahe* # 63, 2008.
[49] First published in *LiNQ*, May, 2009/ also as note 27 above.
ki a – dear [Maori]
[50] First published in *Landfall* # 218, November 2009.
Taku papa – my Father; *pipi* – shellfish [Maori]
[51] First published in *brief*, # 41, 2010.
[52] First published in *Shot Glass Journal*, September 2010.
[53] First published in *Pattaya Poetry Review*, December 2010.
[54] First published in *emanila poetry*, November 2009.
[55] First published by Entropy Press, Auckland, New Zealand, 1987.
[56] First published in *Shot Glass Journal*, September 2010.
[57] First published in *brief*, # 39, March 2010.
[58] First published in *Malaysia Poetry Chronicles*, November 2009.
[59] First published in *Valley Micropress,* August 2011.
[60] First published in *brief* # 40, 2010.
[61] First published in *Auckland Poetry*, October 2010.
[62] As note 27 above.
[63] First published in *a fine line*, February 2011.
[64] As note 27 above.
[65] First published in *brief*, # 40, 2010.

Home, Away, Elsewhere   184

ABOUT PROVERSE HONG KONG

Proverse Hong Kong, co-founded by Gillian and Verner Bickley, is based in Hong Kong with long-term and developing regional and international connections. Verner Bickley has led cultural and educational centres, departments, institutions and projects in many parts of the world. Gillian Bickley has recently concluded a career as a University teacher of English Literature spanning four continents. Proverse Hong Kong draws on their combined academic, administrative and teaching experience as well as varied long-term participation in reading, research, writing, editing, indexing, reviewing, publishing and authorship.

Proverse has published novels, novellas, fictionalized autobiography and biography, non-fiction (including (auto-) biography, diaries, history, memoirs, sport, travel narratives), single-author poetry collections, children's, teens / young adult and academic books. Other interests include academic works in the humanities, social sciences, cultural studies, linguistics and education. Some Proverse books have accompanying audio texts. Some are translated into Chinese.

Proverse welcomes authors who have a story to tell, wisdom, perceptions or information to convey, a person they want to memorialize, a neglect they want to remedy, a record they want to correct, a strong interest that they want to share, skills they want to teach, and who consciously seek to make a contribution to society in an informative, interesting and well-written way. Proverse works with texts by non-native-speaker writers of English as well as by native English-speaking writers.

The name, "Proverse", combines the words "prose" and "verse" and is pronounced accordingly.

There is an informative article on Proverse by Verner Bickley in the November 2011 number of the online literary magazine, Asian Cha, at: www.asiancha.com/content/view/1010/318/

THE PROVERSE PRIZE

The Proverse Prize, an annual international competition for an unpublished book-length work of fiction, non-fiction, or poetry, was established in January 2008. Unusually for a competition of this nature, it is open to all who are at least eighteen on the date they sign the entry form and without restriction of nationality, residence or citizenship.

The objectives of the Proverse Prize are: to encourage excellence and / or excellence and usefulness in publishable written work in the English Language, which can, in varying degrees, "delight and instruct".

Entries are invited from anywhere in the world. Semi-finalists to date include writers born or resident in Andorra, Australia, Canada, Germany, Hong Kong, New Zealand, Nigeria, Singapore, Taiwan, The Bahamas, the PRC, the United Arab Emirates, the United Kingdom, the USA.

Proverse Prize Winners whose books have already been published by Proverse Hong Kong are: Laura Solomon, Rebecca Jane Tomasis, Gillian Jones, David Diskin, Peter Gregoire, Sophronia Liu, Birgit Linder, James McCarthy, Celia Claase, Philip Chatting.

FOUNDERS: Verner Bickley and Gillian Bickley. To celebrate their lifelong love of words in all their forms as readers, writers, editors, academics, performers, and publishers.
HONORARY LEGAL ADVISOR: Mr Raymond T. L. Tse.
HONORARY ACCOUNTANT: Mr Neville Chow.

HONORARY JUDGES: Anonymous.
HONORARY ADVISORS: Bahamian poet Marion Bethel; UK translator, Margaret Clarke; UK linguist & lexicographer David Crystal; Canadian poet and academic, Jonathan Hart; Swedish linguist, Björn Jernudd; Hong Kong University Librarian, Peter Sidorko; Singapore poet and academic, Edwin Thumboo; Czech novelist & poet Olga Walló.
HONORARY UK AGENT AND DISTRIBUTOR: Christine Penney
HONORARY ADMINISTRATORS: Proverse Hong Kong

The Prize
1) Publication by Proverse Hong Kong, with
2) Cash prize of HKD10,000 (HKD7.80 = approx. US$1.00)

If there are two winners, they will share the cash prize and both will be published.
Supplementary publication grants may be made to selected other entrants for publication by Proverse Hong Kong.

Summary Terms and Conditions

Please refer to the year-specific Proverse Prize Entry Form & Terms & Conditions, which are uploaded, no later than 14 April each year, to the Proverse Hong Kong website: <www.proversepublishing.com>.

The free Proverse E-Newsletter includes ongoing information about the Proverse Prize. To be put on the E-Newsletter mailing-list, email: info@proversepublishing.com with your request.

Enquiries by email to <info@proversepublishing.com>.

THE EDITING EXPERIENCE

Winners and Joint-Winners of the Proverse Prize as well as Winners of Supplementary Prizes work with a member of the Proverse Editorial Team to finalise their entered work for publication.

KEY DATES FOR THE AWARD OF THE PROVERSE PRIZE IN ANY YEAR (subject to confirmation in any year)

Receipt of Entry Fees/Forms begins	[Variable, no later than] 14 April - 31 May
Receipt of entered manuscripts begins	1 May - 30 June
Announcement of semi-finalists	August-September of the year of entry
Announcement of finalists	October-December of the year of entry
Announcement of winner/max two winners	March / April to November of the year that follows the year of entry
Cash award Made	At the same time as publication of the winning work(s)
Publication of winning book(s)	Within the period, beginning in November of the year that follows the year of entry

---

POETRY PUBLISHED BY PROVERSE

Following Vaughan Rapatahana's "Home, Away, Elsewhere", you may also enjoy the following single-author poetry collections published by Proverse.

Chasing Light, by Patricia Glinton Meicholas. November 2013.

China Suite and other Poems, by Gillian Bickley. November 2009.

For the Record and other Poems of Hong Kong, by Gillian Bickley. 2003.

Frida Kahlo's Cry and other Poems, by Laura Solomon, 2015.

Heart to Heart, by Patty Ho. 2010.

Home, Away, Elsewhere, by Vaughan Rapatahana.

Immortelle and Bhandaaraa Poems, by Lelawattee Manoo-Rahming. 2011.

In Vitro, by Laura Solomon. 2nd ed. 2013.

Irreverent Poems for Pretentious People, by Henrik Hoeg, 2016.

Moving House and other Poems from Hong Kong, by Gillian Bickley. 2005.

Of Leaves & Ashes, by Patty Ho. 2016.

Of Symbols Misused by Mary-Jane Newton. March 2011.

Painting the Borrowed House: Poems, by Kate Rogers. 2008.

Perceptions, by Gillian Bickley. 2012.

Rain on the Pacific Coast, by Elbert Siu Ping Lee. 2013.

refrain, by Jason S. Polley. 2010.

Shadow Play, by James Norcliffe. 2012.

Shadows in Deferment, by Birgit Bunzel Linder. 2013.

Shifting Sands, by Deepa Vanjani. 2015.

Sightings: a collection of poetry, with an essay, 'Communicating Poems', by Gillian Bickley. 2007.

Smoked Pearl: Poems of Hong Kong and Beyond, by Akin Jeje (Akinsola Olufemi Jeje). 2010.

Unlocking, by Mary-Jane Newton. November 2013.

Wonder, Lust & Itchy Feet, by Sally Dellow. 2011.

POETRY – CHINESE LANGUAGE

For the Record and other Poems of Hong Kong, by Gillian Bickley. Translated into Chinese by Simon Chow. 2010. E-bk.

Moving House and other Poems from Hong Kong, translated into Chinese, with additional material, by Gillian Bickley. Edited by Tony Ming-Tak Yip. Translated by Tony Yip & others. 2008.

WRITE TO US!

We are interested to read your comments on
Vaughan Rapatahan's, *Home, Away, Elsewhere.*
Write to our email address, info@proversepublishing.com,
giving us a few sentences
which you are willing for us to publish,
describing your response to this book.
If your comments are chosen to be included
in our E-Newsletter or website,
we will select another title published by Proverse
and send you a complimentary copy.
When you write to us, please include your name,
email address and correspondence address.
Unless you state otherwise, we will assume that we may cut
or edit your comments for publication.
We will use your initials to attribute your comments.

FIND OUT MORE ABOUT OUR AUTHORS
BOOKS, EVENTS, AND THE PROVERSE PRIZE

Visit our website
http://www.proversepublishing.com

Visit our distributor's website
<www.chineseupress.com>

Follow us on Twitter
Follow news and conversation: <twitter.com/Proversebooks>
OR
Copy and paste the following to your browser window and
follow the instructions: https://twitter.com/#!/ProverseBooks

"Like" us on www.facebook.com/ProversePress

Request our E-Newsletter
Send your request to info@proversepublishing.com.

Availability
Most titles are available in Hong Kong and world-wide
from our Hong Kong based Distributor,
The Chinese University Press of Hong Kong,
The Chinese University of Hong Kong, Shatin, NT,
Hong Kong SAR, China. Web: chineseupress.com

All titles are available from Proverse Hong Kong
and the Proverse Hong Kong UK-based Distributor.

We have stock-holding retailers in Hong Kong,
Singapore (Select Books),
Canada (Elizabeth Campbell Books),
Principality of Andorra (Llibreria La Puça, La Llibreria).
Orders can be made from bookshops in the UK and elsewhere.

Ebooks: Most of our titles are available also as Ebooks.